MW00436040

WALK IN GOD'S GRACE: FAITH FOR FELONS

A 21-DAY DEVOTIONAL

MONICA LYNNE FOSTER

AARON FRANKLIN

ML FOSTER CONSULTING, LLC

Copyright © 2021 by ML Foster Consulting, LLC

Monica Lynne Foster and Aaron Franklin

Cover Design by Jessica Tilles of TWA Solutions.com

All rights reserved. No part of this book may be reproduced in any form without permission from the Publisher at www.monicalynnefoster.com. Please do not participate in or encourage piracy of copyrighted materials in violation of the author's rights. Purchase only authorized editions.

First Edition: June 2019

Scriptures quotations marked (CEB) are from the Common English Bible

Scripture quotations marked (ESV) are from the English Standard Version of the Bible

Scripture quotations marked (GNT) are from the Good News Translation of the Bible

Scripture quotations marked (KJV) are from the King James Version of the Bible

Scripture quotations marked (MSG) are from the Message Translation of the Bible

Scripture quotations marked (NIV) are from the New International Version of the Bible

Scripture quotations marked (NKJV) are from the New King James Version of the Bible

Scripture quotations marked (NLT) are from the New Living Translation of the Bible

Scripture quotations marked (YLT) are from the Youngs Literal Translation of the Bible

ISBN: 0-9965825-9-2

ISBN-13: 978-0-9965825-9-9

The names, places, and incidents within are the products of Aaron's real experiences and the authors' insights. Any resemblance to actual persons, living or dead, business establishments, events, or location are entirely coincidental. The publisher does not have any control over and does not assume any responsibility for author or third-party websites or their content.

If you purchase this book without a cover, you should be aware that this book is stolen property. Neither the author nor the publisher has received any payment for this "stripped book".

We dedicate this book to our mother, Visel J. Franklin.
Our mother always supports us, and she will forever have our love.
Love, Aaron and Monica

⁓

I dedicate this book to my two beautiful children, my daughter Aeryn
and my son Jalen. I know being separated this past year has been
difficult for all of us, but God has a plan. He hasn't forgotten about us,
and we'll be back together soon.
Love, Dad

TABLE OF CONTENTS

WHY WE WROTE THIS BOOK - MONICA

a few years ago — heck, a year ago — it would have been hard for you to tell me I would be writing a book about faith for those who have been or are currently incarcerated. Seriously? I mean, my brother, my twin as my husband likes to call us even though Aaron is eight years my junior, finally had his life together.

I realize that some people are genuinely bad people; walking evil because they choose to be evil. But that's different from most people in our prisons and jail systems. Many people can look back at why they are sitting behind bars and know that they got caught up in an emotional moment. One bad decision has changed the course of their lives, and the lives of those who love them, forever.

That's Aaron, my close-as-twins brother. The one for whom I stayed on my knees constantly before God praying that he would "get it". That he would wake up and understand how much God loves him and how his life could be so much better than what it was. But he was unable to see it for himself. And the cycle of messed up choices and skating by with a slap on the wrist consequences continued to build. Decades went by and the cycle never changed — until June 2, 2018.

That's when it seems that God said, "Aaron, enough is enough! I love you and if you are ever going to live the good life that I've already laid out for you, you are going to have to stop playing games with Me. I want your undivided attention and I'm going to take what could have been a tragedy and use it to turn your life around. And while I'm at it, I'm going to use you to help others." Yep. That's what happened on June 2nd.

Now, in the natural realm, it looked differently. In the natural, there was a gun. A struggle. A shooting. A trial. A conviction. A sentence. A devastation that rippled throughout the family. Faith that was shaken at the very core of those who say they know God and can trust Him through anything.

I pause as I type because I'm still trying to wrap my mind around the onslaught of emotions I feel. I'm sad as I try to avoid staying in the place of "why didn't you..." and "if only you had done..." Those thoughts kill my peace, and yet, they are continually fighting for space in my mind.

The weekend after my brother's sentencing and a couple days before he was to be transferred to prison to begin serving his sentence, we had an emotional conversation. You know, I never understood how emotional pain could be so great that it hurt like physical pain. But it can, and that weekend it did. However, it was my brother, a relative baby in Christ, who prayed this amazing prayer over us and the rest of our family. And then the voice of the Lord spoke to me. He said to take what the devil meant to destroy us and use it to reach others. And *Walk in God's Grace: Faith for Felons* was born.

I spent the months leading up to Aaron's sentencing helping him see that he's righteous in God's eyes. And his heart began to truly open to our Lord's goodness. Watching that transformation in his life and listening to him share with me how he was sharing

God's goodness with others, let me know all of us need to know we are righteous in God's eyes.

Are there consequences to poor choices? Yeah, of course. Are some actions so unbelievably horrific that some of those affected will have trouble forgiving? Yeah, of course. Does that mean that if a person declines to forgive you that God won't forgive you? Absolutely...NOT. God loves us (and you are part of "us") because He is good. Not because we (and you are part of "we") are good.

Be blessed and allow the Lord to minister to you.

Monica

WHY WE WROTE THIS BOOK - AARON

$\mathcal{M}$an, I never saw myself sitting in a cell, looking at twelve years. My kids will be grown. My mom and aunt will be in their 80s. My sister will be pushing up on 60, and my brother-in-law on 70. That night plays in my head like it's on a loop.

I thought my son was in trouble. I did what a father is supposed to do. Dude pulled out on me. I wanna be mad at God, but... I mean, really it ain't even His fault. I get that now. I'm still believing the appeal will get me home and back to my family.

I don't wanna lose myself in here. Prison is hard and would be even harder without support from my family. It's some wicked stuff around me every day, not just in the physical, but also in the spiritual. I don't want to do anything that will extend my stay. It's just a lot of time to think and if I think too long on the wrong things, everything turns bad. And that's no good.

When my sister told me how God wanted us to write this book, I unsure about doing it. Then in the middle of my quarantine, when I felt I was at my breaking point, with my mind playing tricks on me, she sent me the cover. And it's like, in a moment, God pulled me back. Got my mind focused. Reminded me that even though prison feels like I'm in hell, it could always be worse, and God is always with me. And I knew we had to put this book out.

My sister is straight-laced, like she didn't grow up in Detroit with me. But even though my mother did what she could to keep me out of trouble, I let the streets raise me. Now, I'm letting God undo what the devil did. I really started reading my Bible when I was in County. My sister sent me books by Creflo Dollar, and God started talking to me. He had probably been talking all along, but now I was listening. He said I had to forgive myself, because the guilt was killing me. I had to stay strong for my family because they needed me. Man, I can feel Him changing me.

I thought it would be cool to share what I'm living through and maybe it will help someone else. We may be in here for different reasons, but the bottom line is we're in here together. And I don't know one dude who wants to make a return trip when he gets out. I needed some peace. Writing this book helped me get that peace. Now I'm passing it on to you.

Stay strong and do what I'm learning to do. Let go and let God do what God does.

Peace,

Aaron

A LETTER FROM MOM

I am so proud of my children for seeing the need for this book. They have always been able to make lemonade out of lemons, but this is the largest pitcher of lemonade they have ever made!

When the judge declared "12 years" that day in court, I have to admit I was asked to leave the courtroom. It was just so unfair. How could the jury have believed Aaron had done this thing? I ranted and raved about the injustice of it all, the lying that had taken place on the stand, and what I saw as the misconduct of the prosecutor. How could the judge miss seeing what was clear?

Over time, I came to understand that some of this was Aaron's fault; not the verdict, but the situation in which our family found itself. Aaron has always been a child of God, but he had gotten into the habit of ignoring the voice of the Holy Spirit. He told me after the incident, that something had told him to get out of the house. Monica asked him if that was the first time the Spirit had spoken to him during this particular situation. He told her He'd heard the spirit before, but he disregarded the voice.

This is another example of how God wants to take care of His children. Even after Aaron had ignored the voice, the Holy Spirit spoke to him again, and this time, Aaron listened. But it was too late. Things spiraled out of control, and now my son is locked up.

I kept asking God why He let this happen; what good could come of Aaron being in prison? I believe this book is the answer. During his incarceration, Aaron has drawn closer to God, and has found peace in his situation. And in researching the Bible for this book, his trust and faith in God has become stronger. Monica and I have also found our peace concerning this situation.

I pray that the faith of those who read this book be strengthened, that their trust in God will grow, and they will feel a new hope.

Praying for you,
Jeanne Franklin

MAXIMIZE YOUR DEVOTION TIME

*O*ver the next twenty-one days, Aaron and I, through the inspiration of the Holy Spirit, will share some powerful truths with you. It is our prayer that if you can really receive what we are saying, you just might experience the most peace you have felt in a long time.

Each day we will share a devotion with a typical inmate situation and then offer scriptures to help you find peace in those types of situations. We offer a prayer rooted in God's Word that can be prayed at any time, but feel free to pray however you feel God is leading you. Finally, we give you space to journal your thoughts and meditate on the Word.

Allow God to speak directly to you. He loves you and He wants the best for you. He wants you to be at peace, regardless of where you are. He wants you to know how to control your emotions. He wants you to know that you have guardian angels sent to protect you.

We want the truth of His Word to become firmly established in you because that is when the power of God's Word can, and will, absolutely transform your life!

VERSIONS OF THE BIBLE

*I*n this devotion, we use different translations of the Bible. We do this because different versions drive home the points that we are emphasizing in each scripture.

If you have access to multiple versions of the Bible, we encourage you to read and compare translations because you may find that one translation works better for you than another.

Behind each scripture we put the abbreviation of the translation used.

- AMP - Amplified
- CEB - Common English Bible
- ESV - English Standard Version
- GNT - Good News Translation
- KJV - King James Version
- MSG - Message Translation
- NIV - New International Version
- NKJV - New King James Version
- NLT - New Living Translation
- YLT - Youngs Literal Translation

PART I
GOD IS YOUR FRIEND

When we see God as our friend, rather than some abstract mystical being, our relationship with Him changes for the better.

Think about what it means to have a true friend who loves us. We trust that person. We know that because that person loves us, we are forgiven when we make mistakes. A true friend who loves us will gladly have our backs.

Have you ever had a friend who loved you and was with you when everyone (including you) knew you had messed up? Maybe your friend even tried to talk some sense into you. But regardless of whether you listened, that person remained your friend and still supported you. Now, maybe that person is putting money on your books. :-)

Well, these are all the qualities of God. He loves us. He always has our backs. He forgives our mistakes. And He's always depositing into our spiritual accounts.

Imagine how your relationship with God will grow when you begin to see Him as *your* best friend who loves you no matter what!

BELIEVE GOD LOVES YOU

But God demonstrates His own love for us in this: While we were still
sinners, Christ died for us.
Romans 5:8 (NIV)

*B*arry replayed the judge's parting shots in his mind
after he had been sentenced to life without possibility
of parole. "You are a danger to the community. You took an innocent life and I'm going to make sure you never get the opportu-
nity to do it again."

Barry had glanced around the courtroom and saw tears in the
eyes of the victim's mother, who had lost her only child. Next to
her was her only grandson. Barry knew what hate looked like.
That was the look he saw on the face of the victim's father. He
kept looking around hoping that someone from his family was
there for his sentencing. Then he thought, "Why would they be?
They hadn't been there for the trial."

He thought he knew what it felt like to be alone. But sitting in quarantine after sentencing, he felt such a loneliness that he wondered if he should just end it all now.

When my father and my mother forsake me, then the Lord will take care of me.
Psalms 27:10 (NKJV)

But God's mercy is so abundant, and His love for us is so great, that while we were spiritually dead in our disobedience He brought us to life with Christ. It is by God's grace that you have been saved.
Ephesians 2:4-5 (GNT)

Humble yourselves, therefore, under God's mighty hand, that He may lift you up in due time. Cast all your anxiety on Him because He cares for you.
1 Peter 5:6-7 (NIV)

No, in all these things we are more than conquerors through Him who loved us. For I am convinced that neither death nor life, neither angels nor demons, neither the present nor the future, nor any powers, neither height nor depth, nor anything else in all creation, will be able to separate us from the love of God that is in Christ Jesus our Lord.
Romans 8:37-39 (NIV)

The Bible is full of encouraging verses that tell us how much God loves us. When we have done something so awful that it's hard to imagine anyone loving us, know that He does. Think about this; all of our sins were future sins when Jesus died on the Cross. He took the punishment for every wrong turn we would make more than two thousand years later. It is up to us to let God in and allow Him to fill us with His love.

Whatever anxiety, sadness, or depression we may feel, God says to give it to Him. He cares for us. He loves us. He wants us to be well, no matter where we sit, no matter what we've done. God is good to us because He is good, not because we are good.

We love because God first loved us.
1 John 4:19 (GNT)

Grace Walk Prayer

Lord, thank you for telling me in Your Word that You love me. Thank you that even though I did *(fill in the blank)*, that is still not enough for You to turn Your back on me. Lord, because You love me, I am giving You all of my cares. Because You love me, I will stop worrying about *(fill in the blank with whatever is weighing heavily on you)* and give it to You. Because You love me, I know that You will continue to protect me. Because You love me, I can live in peace, no matter where I am. In Jesus' name, I receive Your love for me. Amen.

Grace Walk Thoughts

What is one way that God has shown me lately that He loves me?

GOD FORGIVES

Repent therefore and turn back, that your sins may be blotted out, so that times of refreshing may come from the presence of the Lord
Acts 3:19 (ESV)

*S*olomon was sentenced to life for murder. It was a fair sentence because he was guilty — high on drugs at the time he committed the crime. He's sober now (except for the occasional pruno), and he wants to live a better life, even if it is behind bars. When he was a child, his grandmother would drag him to Sunday School, which he hated. But now he wants to have a relationship with God. Only he wonders what kind of God would be able to forgive him when he finds it difficult to forgive himself.

Prisons are filled with thousands of "Solomons". We encourage you to read Acts 3. Two of the apostles, Peter and John, spoke the authority of Jesus over a man who'd never walked a day in his life, and the man was immediately healed.

The people at the temple witnessed the miracle and were

amazed. These were the same people who had wanted Jesus killed and had asked for a murderer to be released instead of Jesus (Matthew 27:15-25).

Peter spoke to the people and prayed for them. He let them know that God was standing by, waiting for them to repent so He could not only erase their sins, but also send "refreshing".

What does "refreshing" mean anyway? Why is this such a big deal? We're glad you asked. When people are refreshed it means they have been reinvigorated and new life has been breathed into them. That is what Jesus promises to us when we repent from any and all of our sins and give our lives to Him. We are refreshed and we are forgiven.

Side note: If a murderer who was sentenced to death was granted freedom could it be possible that if you truly gave your life to God, the same favor could be shown to you? Just something to think and pray about.

Grace Walk Prayer

Lord, thank you for forgiving me of the sin(s) I committed when I did *(fill in the blank with whatever sin(s) you are asking God to blot out)*. I acknowledge that it was wrong and from this day forward, I want to live my life for You. The way You forgave those who placed You on the Cross, is the way I'm asking You to forgive me. In Jesus' name, I pray. Amen.

Grace Walk Thoughts

Would I feel peace in my life if God forgave me? Would I be able to forgive myself, if I haven't already?

KNOWING GOD

But anyone who does not love does not know God, for God is love.
1 John 4:8 (NLT)

*D*ominic was serving a light sentence. The jail had plenty of Bibles laying around, so he took one and started reading it to pass the time. As he read, he became confused. In the Old Testament he read about this God who rained fire on people and turned a woman into a pile of salt because she took one last look at her home — a home she was forced to leave. Then he read in the New Testament about this God who was healing people and talking about love. So, who was God — fire and brimstone or love? Becoming frustrated, he put the Bible down and didn't pick it up again.

Dominic's story is familiar to anyone who reads the Bible without knowing and understanding the nature and character of God. I (Monica) remember asking God what it meant to "know Him"? I distinctly recall Him asking me a question. (And yes, God talks to me just as He talks / will talk to you.)

Anyway, He asked me what I knew about my mother. I thought that was a strange question, but I said I knew her favorite color, what kind of animals she liked, where she's lived, her profession, her birthdate, etc. He then asked me what I knew about one of my aunts and I was unable to give many specifics. I knew she liked dogs, but that was about it.

When God asked me to consider what made the difference, I said it's the time that I've spent with each of them. My mother and I have a close relationship. We talk almost daily, and I have a genuine interest in her life. Though I love my aunt, it has been almost twenty years since I've actually seen her, and we talk maybe once every five years or so.

The answer is clear. We get to know God by spending time with Him and reading His Word — by talking *with* Him and not just *to* Him. It's a relationship that is cultivated over time. He wants us to know that, yes, He is the God of the Old Testament and He did kill people who disobeyed His law. BUT we are now living in a time where Jesus has paid the ultimate price for our sins, and God allows us to enjoy the promises of the blessings that He promised to Abraham.

But Christ has rescued us from the curse pronounced by the law. When He was hung on the cross, He took upon Himself the curse for our wrongdoing. For it is written in the Scriptures, "Cursed is everyone Who is hung on a tree." Through Christ Jesus, God has blessed the Gentiles with the same blessing He promised to Abraham, so that we who are believers might receive the promised Holy Spirit through faith.
Galatians 3:13-14 (NLT)

Now come on, any God who would give His only Son so that we can live an abundant life on earth and eternally can only be described as a God of Love.

Grace Walk Prayer

Lord, I desire to know You. I desire to have a close and intimate relationship with You. I invite You to come into my heart and speak to me — messages that are just for me. I open my heart to You and ask You to show me who You are. In Jesus' name, I pray. Amen.

Grace Walk Thoughts

How do I see God? Do I believe that He's love and that He loves me?

GOD PROTECTED CAIN

Then the Lord put a mark on Cain to warn anyone who might try to kill him.
Genesis 4:15 (NLT)

John grew up in a rough neighborhood. He had a mother who loved him, but he thought the gang would give him something more. The gang was willing to let him in on the condition that he shoot a random person. John didn't want to do it, but his own life was on the line if he backed out. So, as the car in which he was riding slowed, he pointed the gun out the window and pulled the trigger, aiming at the old man walking down the street. In the rearview window, he saw the man hit the ground. The gang said he was now part of the family.

Since that day, John has racked up a lot of bodies. And, if he is honest with himself, he wants a different kind of life now. He thinks about talking to God but believes there's no way God would ever listen to him, let alone talk back.

Do you know that God protected the first murderer? It's true. Cain was jealous of his brother, Abel, and killed him. Even though there was a consequence to Cain's actions, God still loved him enough to protect him.

One day Cain suggested to his brother, "Let's go out into the fields." And while they were in the field, Cain attacked his brother, Abel, and killed him. Afterward the Lord asked Cain, "Where is your brother? Where is Abel?" "I don't know," Cain responded. "Am I my brother's guardian?" But the Lord said, "What have you done? Listen! Your brother's blood cries out to Me from the ground! Now you are cursed and banished from the ground, which has swallowed your brother's blood. No longer will the ground yield good crops for you, no matter how hard you work! From now on you will be a homeless wanderer on the earth." Cain replied to the Lord, "My punishment is too great for me to bear! You have banished me from the land and from Your presence; You have made me a homeless wanderer. Anyone who finds me will kill me!" The Lord replied, "No, for I will give a sevenfold punishment to anyone who kills you." Then the Lord put a mark on Cain to warn anyone who might try to kill him.
Genesis 4:8-15 (NLT)

Notice how comfortable Cain was in talking to God? I (Monica) believe Cain was having an audible conversation with God. When God asks Cain the whereabouts of his brother, Cain cops an attitude. Can you imagine how you would act if one day, you heard God's voice as clearly as you hear your own? Would you be so informal that you'd be comfortable enough to lie to God? Well, Cain was.

Even though Cain lied to God, got smart with God, and was punished by God, when he told God that he was afraid for his life, God said that anyone who killed Cain would receive a punishment seven times worse than the one He had given Cain.

Then, God sealed His protection of Cain by marking him so everyone would know. Wow. (And no one killed him.)

It's the same for us. When we have a relationship with God, we can talk to Him and He hears and speaks back to us. Even when we have to pay the price for our sins, He still allows us to walk in His protection. Today, God has marked His children by sending the Holy Spirit to live on the inside of us and commanding His angels to protect us.

Welcome Him into your heart and allow Him to do for you what He did for Cain.

Grace Walk Prayer

Lord, I thank You for Your love and protection. Even though I did *(fill in the blank with whatever wrong you're bringing to God right now)* and I have/had to pay my debt to society, I am grateful that You have sealed me with Your Holy Spirit and that Your angels have been dispatched to keep me safe (Psalms 91:11-11-12). As I sleep in my cell or sleep *(fill in the blank with wherever you are)*, You are with me. When I am eating, You are with me. When I'm interacting with anyone, You are with me. Just as You protected Cain, You are protecting me, and I walk in the grace of Your protection. In Jesus' name, I pray. Amen.

Grace Walk Thoughts

Have I ever thought about how God will protect me no matter what I've done? If I can believe that, how will it change my life?

GOD WILL KEEP YOU ON THE RIGHT PATH

Our purpose is to do what is right, not only in the sight of the Lord, but
also in the sight of others.
2 Corinthians 8:21 (GNT)

Screw it. I (Aaron) shouldn't be here and I'm angry. I'm going to do what I see everyone else doing — I'm taking another cookie. I want two cookies and I'm taking the two cookies.

But Big Betty saw it differently. She saw me take that cookie and called me out about it — loudly! I felt like the biggest turd ever. Reason being, I always get extra food just by asking. Stealing was out of my character and God checked me on that immediately. All I could say was never again! (LOL)

God loves His children, and that love is the reason He will keep us on the right path. Now, He also gives us free will, and He will never force us to obey Him.

I am now giving you the choice between life and death, between God's blessing and God's curse, and I call heaven and earth to witness the choice you make. Choose life. Love the Lord your God, obey Him and be faithful to Him, and then you and your descendants will live long in the land that He promised to give your ancestors, Abraham, Isaac, and Jacob.
Deuteronomy 30: 19-20 (GNT)

It is to our benefit to allow God to correct us when we stray from the path that He has set before us. Let's be very clear; in this life, the devil will always lurk around you — always! The devil wants you to make the wrong choices.

He showed us that in Genesis when he tempted Eve to eat from the tree that God expressly told Adam and Eve not to touch or they would die (Genesis 2:17; Genesis 3:1-11). The devil is subtle in his tactics and while God is talking to you and trying to keep you on track or get you back on track, the devil is telling you how much fun you can have doing what is wrong.

What is so awesome about our God is that He knew we would have this battle in life, and He tells us the beautiful promise:

Lo, I have stood at the door, and I knock; if anyone may hear My voice, and may open the door, I will come in unto him, and will sup with him, and he with Me.
Revelation 3:20 (YLT)

Even if we are in prison, God will still come to use if we invite Him into our lives. He will keep us from straying if we just allow Him to do what He does best and that is to love us.

Grace Walk Prayer

Lord, I thank you that you will keep me on the right path if I give my will to you. So today, I purpose in my heart to allow You to take over. Show me how to live and be in peace, regardless of where I am in this very moment and regardless of what may be happening around me. Lord, close my eyes, ears, and heart to anything that goes against You and Your will for my life. In Jesus' name, I pray. Amen.

Grace Walk Thoughts

Why has the devil been trying to get my attention lately? Am I willing to allow God to show me how to navigate around whatever is trying to knock me off my path?

PART II
YOU ARE NOT ALONE

You know what makes solitary confinement so awful? It deprives a person of a basic need — human contact. As human beings, we weren't designed to life in be isolation.

But what if we told you that even if you are physically by yourself, there is still someone with you? It's true. God, in His infinite wisdom and mercy has blessed us with the Holy Spirit and angels that are always with us. Can we see them with our physical eyes? No. Rarely do angels make visible appearances. But they are still real.

We want to spend a couple days sharing scriptures that tell us about our unseen partner and our guardian angels. This is completely life changing and transforming when we understand that God has not left us alone.

YOUR UNSEEN PARTNER

And I will pray the Father, and He will give you another Helper, that He may abide with you forever...
John 14:16 (NKJV)

*A*udra hated church. Everybody was a hypocrite, and the Bible was outdated and confusing. She failed to understand why the jail had so many Bibles laying around, but out of boredom she picked one up and began reading. Yup, it still didn't make any sense.

You may have read today's scriptures and thought the same thing. What in the heck is God trying to say? For that matter, the entire Bible may seem that way to you. But since you're reading this devotional, then you have at least a curiosity.

John 14 (and we encourage you to read this chapter) takes place after Jesus died on the Cross and conquered death. Jesus tells us before He ascends into heaven that it is time for Him to go, but He has prayed and asked God to send us a Helper. A Helper that will live on the inside of us forever and teach us everything we need to know about how to live in this life. So, umm, what exactly does that mean? It means that wherever we are, when we are confused about what to do, we can ask the Holy Spirit (the Helper living within us) to give us guidance.

Have you ever been somewhere and felt something on the inside of you telling you "don't go there" or "take the freeway today instead of the side streets" or "don't steal that cookie, the guards will see you"? When this happens, the Holy Spirit is talking to you, guiding you away from trouble.

The day that changed my life in 2018, I (Aaron) had a feeling that something was wrong. Some call it a feeling in their gut. Some call it intuition. But I know that it was the Holy Spirit. I ignored the warning and found myself in the middle of an ambush. I sometimes sit in my cell and think about where I'd be if I'd just listened.

The more we lean on the Holy Spirit for guidance in every area of our lives, the smoother our lives will be. We can ask Him where to apply for jobs and how to make money to take care of our families. He will tell us which guards are cool and which ones to avoid. He will even let us know who wants to trade soups. (You know what I'm talking about! LOL.) We have this amazing Helper waiting for us to talk to Him and He wants us to listen to the wisdom He has for us.

Will it feel strange at first? Probably. But once you get into the habit of listening to the Holy Spirit, you will wonder how you ever lived this life without Him.

Grace Walk Prayer

Lord, I open my heart to receive the Holy Spirit today. Help me to know Your will for everything that pertains to my life. Lead me in the direction of Your Word and keep me on the path that You have already prepared for me. Thank You for sending me a Helper. In Jesus' name, I pray. Amen.

Grace Walk Thoughts

What is something that I need the Holy Spirit to reveal to me? I will write it down and believe that He will do it.

YOUR GUARDIAN ANGELS

*And he answered, Fear not: for they that be with us are more than they
that be with them. And Elisha prayed, and said, Lord, I pray thee, open
his eyes, that he may see. And the Lord opened the eyes of the young
man; and he saw: and, behold, the mountain was full of horses and
chariots of fire round about Elisha.*
2 Kings 6:16-17 (KJV)

*D*esmond was basically a good kid who made a couple
wrong turns in life and ended up with a five-year
prison sentence. He was new to prison life, and even though he
would avoid admitting it, he was scared. He was a loner but his
bunkie told him that he had to join a gang. Otherwise, the chance
that he would make it to the end of his sentence was slim.
Desmond needed protection and gangs offered that.

In 2 Kings 6, the king of the Syrian army was at war with
Israel. But every time the king of Syria planned an attack against
Israel, it seemed that Israel was warned, and the plans failed. The
king of Syria was certain there was a traitor in his midst that was

telling Israel his war plans. But there was no traitor, only a man of God, Elisha, who heard from God the king's plans and would tell Israel so they could be spared an ambush. The Syrian king was furious and sent his army to kill Elisha.

Elisha and his servant walked outside the next morning to find themselves surrounded by the Syrian army and the servant became afraid. Wouldn't you? Well, Elisha wasn't. Why? Because he knew God had sent His angels to protect him.

Elisha prayed and asked God to open his servant's eyes so he could see what Elisha knew existed without seeing. God's angels had the Syrian army, Elisha's enemies, surrounded. These angels weren't cute little chubby babies with wings. No. These angels were warriors on horses and chariots. They were not to be messed with at all.

There are other scriptures that show angels coming to the aid of God's children. For example, in the New Testament, an angel freed Peter from jail (Acts 12:1-11).

I (Monica) have a personal experience with angels. Years ago, when I was in my twenties, I was visiting a boyfriend at his home, failing to realize that he was cheating on me. Well, his new "boo" showed up with her girls and they wanted to jump me. I was literally backed into a corner, staring at three or four big girls, when all of a sudden, I felt like I was enclosed in a bubble. I could see the girls swinging, but they couldn't touch me. It was a crazy night.

I could share other experiences where God's angels were with me, but my point is to let you know that angels are real. They are waiting to move on your behalf. Hebrews 1:14 tells us they are spirits of service, sent to minister to those who are about to inherit salvation (and that's us).

In *Your Tool Bag* in the back of this devotion, we've shared a list of scriptures that tell you about your angels. If you are incarcerated, then you know that evil is around you 24/7. It is important — maybe even life and death critical — to understand that

YOU have angels who have been commanded by God to protect you. But YOU have to ask God to do it. And He will.

Grace Walk Prayer

Lord, I thank You for the angels that have been sent by You to protect me. I thank You Lord, that Your Word says they will deliver me from trouble. Every day of my life, I walk with my angels and my unseen partner, the Holy Spirit and I know that I am safe. In Jesus' name, I pray. Amen.

Grace Walk Thoughts

If I can believe that angels will watch over me and protect me, would it give me a greater level of peace to deal with where I am at this very moment?

PART III
WALK IT OUT

The last week was about laying a foundation for the Grace Walk that God wants us to take while we are here on earth. It is a journey that you will be on for the rest of your life, just as we are.

Over the next two weeks there will be fourteen devotions that will help get you started on your walk. Or maybe you are already on the journey and these will help lead you further down the road.

YOU ARE AN HEIR

So that thou art no more a servant, but a son, and if a son, also an heir of God through Christ.
Galatians 4:7 (YLT)

Imagine that you were the son or daughter of the Royals in England, or even North West, daughter of Kim and Kanye West. Or how about Blue Ivy, Jay Z and Beyonce's daughter? You would be set for life. Your name alone would get you into "members only" events. You would have private jets and access to the best things that money could buy. But what the money would not guarantee, is a life full of hope, joy, and peace.

In Galatians, we learn that we are much more than just servants of God. We are His sons and daughters, and because we are His children, we are heirs! Many people will read this in the Bible and fail to understand the power of this blessing of God.

EVERYTHING that God owns belongs to us because we are

His adopted children. Everything. That God owns. Belongs. To. US.

So, what does God own? Psalms 50:12 tells us that the world belongs to God and the fullness thereof. The world and the fullness thereof also belong to those of us who have made Jesus our Lord and Savior — those of us who are God's adopted children.

Daniel 2:20 tells us that wisdom and power belong to God. Guess what? Wisdom and power belong to us as well. James 1:5 confirms that God gives wisdom liberally to everyone who asks for it. God has given us the matchless name of Jesus that allows us to walk in a level of authority that many Christians don't even know about, let alone know how to operate.

Many times in the Bible, you will see the word "Selah." It means "to pause and calmly think of that." Selah on this point: As God's children, we have authority over all the power of the enemy. The bountiful goodness of the earth belongs to us because we belong to Him. We have wisdom in every area of our lives if we just ask for it. Please refrain from letting this knowledge go in one ear and out the other.

Wherever you sit right now, and for however long you will be sitting there, pause on this thought: As God's child, you have authority over every evil that is present around you. You have the ability to ask the Holy Spirit how to navigate your daily living and He will show you.

There may be a day where He tells you by a feeling in your gut, that you should skip chow. Or stay inside rather than go out for yard. Decline that batch of pruno — the COs are planning a shake down and you want to stay out of any mess. Pass on trading with that guy — he's going to try and blackmail you with it. Whatever the circumstance may be, as God's child, YOU have more power and influence than the children of the greatest entertainer or celebrity on earth. Selah.

. . .

Grace Walk Prayer

Lord, I thank You that I am Your adopted child. I look forward to reading more about the benefits of being Your child and walking in Your blessings. What I know at this very moment, is that I have the fruit of the Spirit within me (Galatians 5:22-23). That fruit is love, joy, peace, long-suffering, kindness, goodness, faith, gentleness, and self-control. What I know right now, is that, though I may not be able to control what others do, I have a Helper, the Holy Spirit, navigating me around danger, both seen and unseen. Just as celebrities have bodyguards to watch over them, I have my guardian Angels that keep me safe. I thank you that I am Your beloved child. In Jesus' name, I pray. Amen.

Grace Walk Thoughts

What is the first thing you want to ask your Father now that you know
You are His child?

_____

_____

_____

_____

_____

_____

_____

_____

_____

_____

_____

_____

_____

_____

_____

_____

_____

_____

_____

_____

_____

_____

_____

_____

_____

_____

BE HONEST WITH YOURSELF

Thank God! The answer is in Jesus Christ our Lord. So you see how it
is: In my mind I really want to obey God's law, but because of my sinful
nature I am a slave to sin.
Romans 7:25 (NLT)

here were times in my (Aaron's) life that I did things
and made decisions that, in retrospect, were stupid
and reckless. I would look at my circumstances and think I was
making good decisions and doing the right things.

I thought it was fine to "cut corners" here and there. I thought
there was nothing wrong with being "the middleman." For most
of my adult life that was how I lived, refusing to believe that what
I was doing was wrong. In my mind, I was trying to build for my
family and that was that. I actually felt like it was God who was
blessing me with these different opportunities to make money.
But that's how the devil draws us in. It starts out with something
small, like hooking someone up with a bag of weed to now I'm

moving weight. All the while justifying what I'm doing. Been there? Can you relate?

People, not just inmates, are highly skilled at telling ourselves lies, believing the lies, and then trying to sell those lies to others who aren't buying. We give ourselves the benefit of the doubt and justify our wrong choices. But if we want to see change begin to take place in our lives, we have to get real with ourselves. We have to judge ourselves the way we would judge others who are doing what we're doing. And hey, the process of being honest with ourselves can be difficult, especially if it's something we're not used to doing. But God tells us:

All Scripture is inspired by God and is useful to teach us what is true and to make us realize what is wrong in our lives. It corrects us when we are wrong and teaches us to do what is right.
2 Timothy 3:16 (NLT)

It is when we allow Jesus to show us the faults of our current thinking, living, behaving, responding, and talking, that we will see the manifestation of God's promises in our lives.

Grace Walk Prayer

Lord, I thank you so much that You love me enough to keep it real with me about how I am as a person. Show me where I have been deceiving myself into thinking that certain things are okay, when really, we both know those things are wrong. I am trusting that You will love me through my transformation, and I look forward to meeting the new and improved version of myself. In Jesus' name, I pray. Amen.

Grace Walk Thoughts

What are some of the lies I've told myself? Am I willing to have God show me how to live a life that is based on being honest with everyone, including myself?

_____

_____

_____

_____

_____

_____

_____

_____

_____

_____

_____

_____

_____

_____

_____

_____

_____

_____

_____

_____

_____

_____

_____

_____

_____

_____

_____

RENEW YOUR MIND

Therefore we must pay much closer attention to what we have heard,
lest we drift away from it
Hebrews 2:1 (ESV)

*H*ow *will you keep the Jesus you found in jail now that*
you're home? That was the question Juan's aunt asked
when he was paroled after spending a year in jail.

Juan's aunt was talking about the phenomenon of felons who
"find Jesus" in prison and then fail to take Jesus with them when
they leave. They turn to God because they are scared and
desperate (even if they don't admit it).

They're scared a trial will go differently than desired. Or
scared about how long their sentence will be. Scared at the
thought of being forgotten by their families. Scared about how to
handle themselves in jail life. It's logical that they would turn to
God. But once they are out and back in a comfortable environment, their days become consumed with routine life and God
gets pushed to the side.

The slide away from God is so subtle, they usually fail to realize they are straying. By the way, this isn't unique to prisoners. Most of us want God to be our best buddy when we're in a jam, and we push Him away once our crisis is over.

I (Monica) asked God about it and He said we do this when we have not renewed our minds.

Don't copy the behavior and customs of this world, but let God transform you into a new person by changing the way you think. Then you will learn to know God's will for you, which is good and pleasing and perfect.
Romans 12:2 (NLT)

Every day as we renew our minds, we should make sure these points remain front and center in our thoughts.

God loves me
But God demonstrates His own love toward us, in that while we were still sinners, Christ died for us.
Romans 5:8 (NKJV)

God has a perfect plan for me
For we are His workmanship, created in Christ Jesus for good works, which God prepared beforehand that we should walk in them.
Ephesians 2:10 (NKJV)

God has promised me good things
I tell you, you can pray for anything, and if you believe that you've received it, it will be yours.
Mark 11:24 (NLT)

God gives me a hope and a future
For I know the thoughts that I think toward you, says the Lord, thoughts of peace and not of evil, to give you a future and a hope.

Jeremiah 29:11 (NKJV)

God has forgiven my sins
And Jesus said to her, "Neither do I condemn you; go and sin no more."
John 8:11b (NKJV)

Whether you are behind bars or outside of them, renew your mind DAILY to these five truths and watch how wonderful your life will be.

Grace Walk Prayer

Lord, I thank You for the promises in Your Word. Your perfect plan for me is that I walk in Your Word every day. I surrender every part of my life to You and I will allow the Holy Spirit to lead me daily. I daily yield my mind, my will, and my emotions to You. I yield to You the way I think. I yield to You the way I feel. I yield to You the choices I make. And with an open heart, I welcome the renewal process that takes place in me every single day and transforms my life for the better. In Jesus' name, I pray. Amen.

Grace Walk Thoughts

Have I thought about renewing my mind? No matter where I am or in what circumstances I find myself, what are three (3) promises of God to me that I can keep in my heart?

THERE IS A WAY THAT SEEMS RIGHT

There's a way of life that looks harmless enough; look again — it leads straight to hell. Sure, those people appear to be having a good time, but all that laughter will end in heartbreak.
Proverbs 14:12-13 (MSG)

ichael grew up conflicted. His mother and father were too young to be parents, and by the time he was born, they were breaking up. Each one moved on to other relationships and had more children.

Michael found himself being raised by a mother who taught him that smoking and selling weed was harmless and a father who taught him that death was better than dishonor in the streets. His grandmother wanted the best for him, however, she was unable to provide consistent discipline with him, while his father was "away" physically, and his mother was "away" emotionally.

Michael found himself having to sift through mixed signals of how he should be living his life. When it was all said and done, he decided that smoking weed as a young teenager and keeping quiet when his friends did wrong, was the right way to live.

Michael's story is common. Parents go away to jail or prison, leaving their children with competing messages of right and wrong. Because no matter how many times children are told, "Do as I say and not as I do," the children are inevitably watching what the parent is doing. To get the messaging right, we must get it right with ourselves.

Have the choices we've made as parents seemed right to us and yet, landed us behind bars? If so, most likely, we will need to rewire our thought processes.

Yesterday, we talked about renewing our minds to what God's Word says. If we have been living our lives in a way that seems right and yet, we are continually finding ourselves in trouble, then maybe — just maybe — we are going the wrong way.

We must weigh every decision we make against the Word of God. If God's Word supports it, then we move forward. If the support is lacking, then we look for a different option. If we are unsure, we pray about it or talk to someone who may be further down the path in Christ than we are.

Our choices impact more than just ourselves. We have to avoid letting our lives be the roadmap to sending our children straight to hell or sitting in a cell beside us.

Grace Walk Prayer

Lord, I admit that I may fail to understand how the choices I make affect my future and the future of my children or future children. Please bring my thoughts and actions into alignment with Your will. That is the only way I will know for sure that I am living a life of blessings and sharing that life with my loved ones. In Jesus' name, I pray. Amen.

Grace Walk Thoughts

How often do I think about what I do before I do it? Have I trained myself to think that ways that are not right, are right? Do I truly know right from wrong?

WHAT A BATTLE WITH AN ENEMY
LOOKS LIKE

Put on all the armor that God gives you, so that you will be able to
stand up against the devil's evil tricks.
Ephesians 6:11 (GNT)

I (Aaron) remember having an issue with a CO up north. I didn't know what I had done to this guy, but he was always on me — constantly shaking me down, shaking down my area of control, and doing other things that weren't cool. This situation went on for a couple of months. I tried talking to other COs about it, but none really seemed to care (big surprise). It got to the point where I contemplated getting physical with him and we know that getting physical with a CO never works out well for us.

Battling people and circumstances in prison is just a part of prison life. We're battling with gangs, bunkies, guards, "the system", family at home, inmates who are having a bad day, having our own bad day. I mean, the list is exhausting. Physically we may get into arguments or even fist fights with other inmates, but I believe most of our battles are spiritual and they manifest into physical violence.

God tells us to put on armor and that is warrior language. And not just any armor. He tells us to put on the armor that *He* gives us. He knows we have to fight. We just have to be clear about who we're fighting.

We're fighting the devil, and he's all around us. He just disguises himself so that we see something or someone else. A lot of people don't believe the devil is real. But failing to believe he exists will lead us to letting our guard down. Included in *Your Tool Bag* is *The Whole Armor of God*, which is Ephesians 6: 11-18.

Back to the issue with that CO. I talked again to one of the other COs who was aware of what was going on, and right after we spoke, the guard with whom I had the issue threw all my property on the floor. I put on my armor from God and I prayed. I was immediately overwhelmed with peace. A calm came over me that I can't explain. The CO I had talked to moved me out of the unit as I had asked and filed a grievance against the first CO. That was God. He fought that battle against a seemingly unbeatable enemy. And God won. (Tomorrow we will talk about how our enemies are already defeated!)

Grace Walk Prayer

Lord, I thank You for giving me the armor that I need to stand against any attack that tries to come against me. Your Word would only tell me to do something if I was able to do it. So, if You tell me that I can stand against the evil tricks of the devil and win, then I believe that I can. In Jesus' name, I pray. Amen.

Grace Walk Thoughts

Who has been baiting me to go against God's will? Am I willing to put on my armor and stand? Do I believe that I can win?

YOUR ENEMIES ARE DEFEATED

*Look, I have given you authority over all the power of the enemy, and
you can walk among snakes and scorpions and crush them. Nothing
will injure you.*
Luke 10:19 (NLT)

*D*ion served his country for ten years. He fought hard
against his country's enemies and led his team well.
He always went into battle with a plan. When he came home, he
made a couple wrong turns in his life and found himself serving
an eight-year prison sentence. Now, he is fighting a different
kind of battle — one that he is less confident he can win.

Think about what you are going through. Maybe a bunkie,
who is the reason you sleep with one eye open. Maybe a guard
who keeps your meds away from you when you need them.
Maybe it's gang wars inside and outside the jail, and you're trying
to avoid getting caught in the middle. You need a plan for
managing your days in jail.

We read in Colossians 2 that Jesus defeated our enemies when

He conquered death on the Cross. And now He has given us the authority to use His Name to defeat our enemies, whomever and wherever they may be. But it only happens when we open our mouths and speak the authority He has given us. That's our infallible plan. Sooooo, how do we do that?

Well, first we **believe**. Believe that God has given us power over our enemies. If we are feeling skeptical, then we must spend more time in the Word. God tells us throughout the Bible that the devil is defeated, but if we disbelieve that, we will be defeated by satan at every turn.

And these signs will accompany those who believe: In My Name they
will drive out demons
Mark 16:17a (NIV)

Next, we **submit** and **resist**. We submit our will to God's will, and we resist the devil and his games. All things (including the devil) have been placed under Jesus' feet and since we are in Jesus, that means that all things (including the devil) are under our feet as well. The more we allow the Word of God to influence our thoughts and actions, the greater our victory over satan.

So then, submit yourselves to God. Resist the devil, and he will run
away from you. Come near to God, and He will come near to you.
James 4:7-8a (GNT)

God has put all things under the authority of Christ and has made Him
head over all things for the benefit of the church
Ephesians 1:22 (NLT)

The God of peace will soon crush Satan under your feet. May the grace
of our Lord Jesus be with you
Romans 16:20 (NLT)

Third, we **speak** *to* our problem not *about* our problem. I (Monica) once heard a minister say that satan is always looking for an earth-suit to inhabit so he can do harm to God's children. If we stop and think about it, have we ever actually seen satan? No. We see the results of his influence.

For instance, when someone commits murder, that is a direct result of satan's influence over that person. When someone curses us, steals our tablet, or takes the roll off our tray, that is satanic influence. Those are all actions designed to anger us and move us away from God's will. BUT, when situations arise and we recognize who's behind it (meaning we see the devil for who he is and what he's doing), we have the authority to speak to that situation and when we are in God's will, He will back our play.

Then Jesus said to the disciples, "Have faith in God. I tell you the truth, you can say to this mountain, 'May you be lifted up and thrown into the sea,' and it will happen. But you must really believe it will happen and have no doubt in your heart. I tell you, you can pray for anything, and if you believe that you've received it, it will be yours."
Mark 11:22-24 (NLT)

Fourth, **remember your guardian angels**. They have been sent here to protect us. If we are without a plan in lockup or anyplace else, we will find ourselves subject to whatever is happening around us and to us. But if we have a plan that starts with God's promises, then He promises us that nothing will hurt us.

For He will order His angels to protect you wherever you go. They will hold you up with their hands so you won't even hurt your foot on a stone.
Psalm 91:11-12 (NLT)

Grace Walk Prayer

Lord, thank You for telling me in Your Word that I have authority over my enemies and that they are defeated. Lord, as I eat, sleep, live, and breathe in this place, I thank you that I have no fear of the evil that's around me. I thank You that (name your issue) is subject to Your Word and that it/they cannot harm me because You will keep me safe. I walk daily in Your victory. In Jesus' name, I pray. Amen.

Grace Walk Thoughts

What or who is an enemy that's bothering me? If I can believe that he, she, or it, is really defeated by the authority Jesus has given to me, how would that make my life easier or better?

_____
_____
_____
_____
_____
_____
_____
_____
_____
_____
_____
_____
_____
_____
_____
_____
_____
_____
_____
_____
_____
_____
_____
_____
_____

GUARD YOUR HEART

Guard Your Heart
For they are life to those who find them, And health to all their flesh.
Keep your heart with all diligence, For out of it spring the issues of life.
Proverbs 4:22-23 (NKJV)

S hawn listened to the guys talking as they worked out.
One was complaining about his bunkie. The other
complained about how he could never get to the phone. Another
complained that his family screwed up his Securepak (a package
that contains food and other items and can only be ordered by a
friend or family member once a quarter). Another was pissed
because he sent a kite (a request) for medical and was still waiting
on a response.

Each complaint was legitimate. At varying times of his incarceration, Shawn had those same issues. It was just part of jail life.
Before prison, Shawn had been upbeat. But now? Well, now he
had trouble focusing on anything positive. God knew that we
would have this battle — staying positive — in our human lives.

You may be in a negative environment, with all kinds of evil around you every hour of every day. BUT you have the ability to create your own personal joy by guarding your heart. Think of your heart as your "thought" life. In this regard, this is different from the physical organ in your chest.

Refuse to allow someone else's stinky day to infect your great day. Keep a positive attitude and either the people around you will be positive — at least in your presence — or they will stay away from you. They may think you're weird. So what? It is more important to "guard your heart" than care about what someone says about you.

Grace Walk Prayer

Lord, I understand that it is important to guard my heart and refuse to let the negative vibes that are around me become a part of me. Please help me in my walk, because I can't do this without you. In Jesus' name, I pray. Amen.

Grace Walk Thoughts

If I'm honest with myself, would I say that I tend to be more positive or negative? Do I allow the negativity around me to infect my thought life and my heart? If so, what changes can I make?

WORDS HAVE POWER

Words Have Power
What you say can preserve life or destroy it; so you must accept the
consequences of your words.
Proverbs 18:21 (GNT)

I (Aaron) had to learn that the words I spoke had power — good and bad. There was a point during my incarceration where my body always felt beaten and broken down. Guys would ask me if I wanted to workout or lift weights with them and I would say something like, "My legs are messed up" or "my back won't let me." Well, guess what? That's exactly what happened. I moved like an old man.

One of the worst sayings that is popular today is, "It is what it is." I cringe when I hear that phrase because it can immediately stop the flow of God's power in the life of whoever says it.

The Word tells us to speak things that are not as though they already are (Romans 4:17). Most of us fail to understand this and as a result, we say whatever comes to mind. When we think something is funny, we'll say, "I was dying." Really? Did laughter almost make us die? Of course not. So why do we say it? Because we don't believe that words have any power.

Once I stopped saying and accepting the negative things I was feeling, the pain went away, and I began to exercise without discomfort. I'm continuing to learn to think before I say something negative and spin it into a positive. It's hard in the beginning because you may be going through a difficult situation, like I am, but believe me when I tell you that it works.

To understand how powerful words really are, we encourage you to read Genesis 1. Notice that before anything appeared, it was first spoken.

You are snared by the words of your mouth, you are taken by the words of your mouth.
Proverbs 6:2 (NKJV)

Grace Walk Prayer

Lord, as I move in this life, please help me to be aware of the words that I speak. Renew my mouth to speak only those words that You would have me say. Help me, Father, to align my mouth to speak only what You want for me. In the name of Jesus, bind up all contrary thoughts. Show me in Your Word, how everything in creation first started with a word. In Jesus' name, I pray. Amen.

Grace Walk Thoughts

How often do I pay attention to what I say? What would my life be like if I began speaking with purpose and intention?

_____
_____
_____
_____
_____
_____
_____
_____
_____
_____
_____
_____
_____
_____
_____
_____
_____
_____
_____
_____
_____
_____
_____
_____
_____
_____
_____

PROTECT YOUR PEACE

Protect Your Peace
Turn away from evil and do good. Search for peace, and work to
maintain it. The eyes of the Lord watch over those who do right, and
His ears are open to their prayers. But the Lord turns His face against
those who do evil.
1 Peter 3:11-12 (NLT)

I (Aaron) was in level 4 and waiting to use the phone when someone jumped in front of me. Now, those of you who have been in level 4 know that getting the phone can be difficult. You've, no doubt, seen what can happen over the phone.

I had a decision to make — allow myself to become angry and let this inmate disturb my peace or remain calm and figure out another way to get to make my calls. I was thankful that another inmate saw what happened and handed me the phone he was using when he was done. Because I kept my peace, I was still able to make the calls I needed to make and stay out of trouble.

Being in an environment like this and trying to protect my

peace can be difficult. There will be inmates and guards who don't understand what I am doing and test me. But it's up to me to maintain the peace that God has given me. I've had many lessons while in here, but one of the greatest is that my incarceration is temporary. It's temporary for most of us in here. That means none of this is going to last.

God's Word has countless scriptures about peace. If I'm honest, my journey trusting in God has been difficult (and that's downplaying it). But what I'm coming to understand is that when I pray for peace from God, I may not feel it right away. Sometimes, it actually feels like He puts me in situations where I have to find my peace myself. But as long as I keep His Word in my face, I will experience a level of peace that only He can provide.

Don't worry about anything; instead, pray about everything. Tell God what you need, and thank Him for all He has done. Then you will experience God's peace, which exceeds anything we can understand. His peace will guard your hearts and minds as you live in Christ Jesus.
Philippians 4:6-7 NLT

Grace Walk Prayer

Lord, only You know how hard it is in here. I am turning to You because I need constant peace in my life. I don't want to feel like I always have to watch over my shoulder. Please let Your peace that passes all of my understanding, cover me like a blanket so that I may rest. In Jesus' name, I pray. Amen.

Grace Walk Thoughts

What has been robbing me of my peace? Have I turned it over to God?

_____
_____
_____
_____
_____
_____
_____
_____
_____
_____
_____
_____
_____
_____
_____
_____
_____
_____
_____
_____
_____
_____
_____
_____
_____
_____
_____
_____
_____

GRACE AND PEACE MULTIPLIED

Grace and Peace Multiplied
Grace and peace be multiplied unto you through the knowledge of God,
and of Jesus our Lord
2 Peter 1:2 (KJV)

*C*arl felt like he was about to lose it on somebody if the guy in the cell next to him kept screaming. All during the night this dude would yell and bang on his cell bars. Carl snapped on him last week and got a ticket. One more ticket and he was going in the hole for thirty days. But if that guy made one more sound...

Been there? So agitated by what is going on around you that you let your emotions take over? Maybe that's what landed you in jail. But God's Word says that He wants grace and peace to be multiplied to you.

What exactly is grace? It is God's unearned and undeserved approval and support.

And peace? It is being free from danger or threat in the midst of confusion and uncertainty.

Multiplied? It is to increase exponentially.

Knowledge of God? It is a familiar, private, and personal connection to and with God.

Peter is telling us that because of Jesus, and because of our familiar, private and personal connection to and with God, we have an exponential increase in our unearned and undeserved approval and support from our Lord. And an exponential increase in our freedom from danger and threat in the midst of confusion and uncertainty. Whew. That's a mouthful! But marinate on that for a moment. When you are faced with a situation that is overwhelming, your intimate relationship with God through Jesus will bring you through.

Getting locked up. Dealing with the politics of jail life. Being away from your family. Dealing with angry, power tripping guards. All of these things can steal your peace. God is showing you how to get it back.

Spend time in His Word. Find scriptures that help you settle down when you feel frustration. It will be your relationship and time spent with God that will navigate you through this stretch of time.

Grace Walk Prayer

Lord, I believe that You truly want me to walk in Your unmerited favor, meaning, You want to show me Your approval above others and this approval is truly undeserved. You want to surround me with Your protection everywhere I go. Lord, let Your Word come alive within me. My life will become transformed and I will live for You. In Jesus' name, I pray. Amen.

Grace Walk Thoughts

*What's been stealing my peace lately? How is God showing me
unmerited favor and providing me with security when I am in trouble?*

_____
_____
_____
_____
_____
_____
_____
_____
_____
_____
_____
_____
_____
_____
_____
_____
_____
_____
_____
_____
_____
_____
_____
_____
_____
_____
_____
_____
_____

MOUNTAIN MINDSET

Mountain Mindset
You keep him in perfect peace, whose mind is stayed on You, because he
trusts in You
Isaiah 26:3 (ESV)

On the count of Assault with Intent to Commit Great Bodily Harm Less than Murder, how do you find the defendant? Guilty. On the count of Home Invasion 1st Degree, how do you find the defendant? Guilty. I (Aaron) didn't hear anything after that, but they tell me the jury said guilty four more times. They also tell me I threw a chair. I lost time for over forty-eight hours and when I came back to myself, I had to ask what day it was.

How did the jury fail to see what was obvious? How did the prosecutor let her witness take the stand and lie? I knew the justice system was about something other than justice — at least for someone who looks like me. But I truly believed that I would win my case. I ain't gonna lie — my faith was rocked.

It's challenging when we feel like we have no hope. When it seems that the light at the end of the proverbial tunnel is nonexistent for us. Whether the system dealt us a crushing blow or whether we actually did the crime, either way, we're doing time. Hoping our families can come up with the money for an appeal, or at least a Securepak because we can only eat just so many plates of potatoes and beans.

So how do we keep our mountain mindset when we're in a valley? God. He is our hope. He is our future. He will give us peace in our times of trouble. God never promised us an easy life. Heck, Jesus had it hard. But what He does tell us is that He is bigger than any storm we will ever face. Even though His work may be invisible to us, He is working for us.

Fast forward to the day of sentencing. Twelve years. This time, I kept my peace. I told my family I'm all right and that I loved them as the deputies walked me out of the courtroom. I told my sister, God must have something He wants me to do, so I'm gonna lace up my boots and keep walking for Him.

When it feels like we are walking alone, He is walking with us. When our circumstances are still overwhelming, our peace can be restored, and our outlook can be bright. We can be a light, no matter where we sit. He sees our pain. He hears our cries. He remembers us and He is always working for us. James 1:12 has seen me (Aaron) through a lot of rough nights.

Happy are those who remain faithful under trials, because when they succeed in passing such a test, they will receive as their reward the life which God has promised to those who love Him.
James 1:12 (GNT)

Grace Walk Prayer

Lord, it is You who sustains me. It is You who gives me life and peace in my times of sorrow. When I feel so weak Lord, it is

You who lifts me high above my troubles. Thank You Lord, that You love me so much that You are seeing me through this turbulent moment in my life. Because of You, Lord, I am able to have a mountain mindset when I'm walking in a valley. Praise be to You and You alone. In Jesus' name, I pray. Amen.

Grace Walk Thoughts

What one thing can I do this week that will help me begin to see myself as walking above my present circumstances?

_____

_____

_____

_____

_____

_____

_____

_____

_____

_____

_____

_____

_____

_____

_____

_____

_____

_____

_____

_____

_____

_____

_____

_____

_____

PRAYER FOR THE GUARDS

Pray for the Guards
I urge you, first of all, to pray for all people. Ask God to help them;
intercede on their behalf, and give thanks for them. Pray this way for
kings and all who are in authority so that we can live peaceful and quiet
lives marked by godliness and dignity. This is good and pleases God our
Savior, who wants everyone to be saved and to understand the truth
1 Timothy 2:1-4 (NLT)

A situation occurred with me (Aaron) while in quarantine.
I had to use the bathroom and was waiting for the CO to
make his rounds. I knew it was going to be a close call. LOL. As
the CO walked toward me, he could see that I really had to go to
the bathroom. But, instead of reaching for his keys to open my
cell, he walked right past me! I said, "CO, I need to get in my crib.
I gotta use the bathroom." His response was that he wasn't
opening cells right then, he was doing rounds only (but in a
different tone).

Initially I was angry and couldn't understand what the big

deal was about opening my cell. It took about an hour for me to get over it. I had to ask God for inner peace and understanding. And He led me to pray for that CO.

Corrections Officers have a very difficult job and sometimes they may react or respond to a situation differently than the way we feel they should. Unfortunately, that CO was assaulted by an inmate later that same day for doing to someone else what he did to me. We, inmates and guards, have to learn to co-exist and have empathy for each other.

In this scripture, Paul makes a case for why we should pray for others. It is so WE can lead quiet and peaceful lives. When we pray for those in authority over us, we will experience less trouble and greater favor with them.

If you're still locked up, you want the guards to make your life as smooth as possible. If you're back on the streets you want to avoid having contact with the law. If you get pulled over while driving, you want to escape harassment. You want peace. If you're going to get a ticket, you want to avoid being back in handcuffs.

It may take some time but work to develop a habit of prayer when it comes to people who can control the amount of freedom you have. Again, if God tells us do something, He will give us the ability to do it. If He is telling us to pray for them, then He will give us the grace to be able to do just that.

Grace Walk Prayer

Lord, I thank You that You give me favor with You and with *(fill in the blank with the name(s) of whoever is giving you problems)*. I pray that *(fill in the blank with the name(s) of whoever is giving you problems)* submits to You when it comes to me. As I move forward, I pray that every interaction I have with *(name(s))* is peaceful and works to my benefit. Lord, I know that *(name(s))* is a person with his/her own set of life challenges. I pray that he/she learns how to give those challenges over to You and that he/she refrains from taking out his/her frustrations on me. I thank You for honoring Your Word. And that instead of adding issues, _(name(s))_ will add to the peace of my life. In Jesus' name, I pray. Amen.

Grace Walk Thoughts

Do I have an officer, judge, parole officer, or someone else who is giving me a hard time? I will write their name(s) and offer up the Grace Walk Prayer for them.

YOUR YOUTH RESTORED

Your Youth Restored
Who satisfies your years with good things, So that your youth is
renewed like the [soaring] eagle.
Psalm 103:5 (AMP)

*A*yana was crushed. Twenty years. That was her sentence. Going in at twenty-one she would be in her forties when she got out. She felt like her life was over.

Ayana's story is familiar to a lot of us. We make mistakes when we are young and lose a lot of our youth. By the time we get ourselves together or get released from prison, years — if not decades — have gone by. Unless we are careful, we will let those twenty years multiply and steal the rest of our lives.

But did you know that before the following people were famous, they made choices that caused them to spend time in and out of jail/prison?

Tim Allen, star of the sitcoms "Home Improvement" and "Last

Man Standing" was reportedly arrested and served time for being caught with over a pound of cocaine.

Mark Wahlberg, now a movie star, was arrested for attempted murder at the age of sixteen. He allegedly pled guilty to assault and received and served part of a two-year sentence.

Danny Trejo, now a movie star, was raised by an uncle who was allegedly an armed robber and addict, and Trejo served five years in prison for selling heroin.

How about Samuel L. Jackson? He says he was forty-five before he did an acting job sober. And that's when his career took off.

There are others, but the point here is that each of these individuals made a choice to let their past actions stay in their past. They made positive changes and moved forward, creating dream careers for themselves.

Psalm 103:5 tells us about the eagles. Maybe you are wondering about the significance of the eagle. Eagles, besides being symbolic of grace, strength, courage, and leadership, go through a fascinating molting process. Eagles can live up to fifty years and when they are old, their feathers, beak and claws wither. They find a secure place from predators and pluck out their wings, break off their beak by smashing it on a rock, and rub off their talons. The eagles that emerge from this process are said to be stronger than they were when they were young.

Think of yourself as someone who has gone or is going through the molting process. Yes, it's tough. But God's Word promises that you will emerge better than you were before.

Grace Walk Prayer

Lord, thank You for restoring the years that the devil is trying to steal from me. I am being renewed during my time of incarceration and I will emerge better, stronger, more focused, and more determined than I've ever been in my life to live my best life. In Jesus' name, I pray. Amen.

Grace Walk Thoughts

If my youth was renewed and I was the strongest I've ever been, what would I do with my life?

_____
_____
_____
_____
_____
_____
_____
_____
_____
_____
_____
_____
_____
_____
_____
_____
_____
_____
_____
_____
_____
_____
_____
_____
_____
_____
_____

YOU. ARE. RIGHTEOUS

*I*n Christian circles, we hear the word "righteous" all the time. Sometimes, words can be said so frequently, that the impact of their meaning becomes watered down. Today, we want you to know why it is so incredible that you are righteous in God's eyes.

To be righteous, means to be justified, acquitted, freed, and vindicated. There is a good chance that you are or were behind bars because you did something that was wrong. Resist thinking that your past action defines who you are as person. If you have given your life to Christ, then you are righteous. You are freed. You are vindicated. You are justified. Why? Because God loves you. Period.

Most people think you have to change your behavior in order to receive the identity of who Jesus says you are. But you need to flip that attitude. It is knowing and accepting who Jesus says you are that will change your behavior.

Yet in all these things we are more than conquerors through Him who loved us. For I am persuaded that neither death nor life, nor angels nor principalities nor powers, nor things present nor things to come, nor

height nor depth, nor any other created thing, shall be able to separate
us from the love of God which is in Christ Jesus our Lord.
Romans 8:37-39 (NKJV)

Know this. The devil is going to oppose you. He will try and tell you that you are something other than what God has promised you. Satan will make your wrongs play on a continual loop in your mind — it's his job. And when you try and walk right and slip up, he will throw it in your face and tell you all kinds of awful things about you. He is trying to create his own narrative about who you are.

Your job is to maintain what Jesus obtained for you. Jesus paid the greatest price that could be paid for your sins. So, whatever your crime — theft, lying, murder, rape, molestation, domestic violence, assault, robbery, gang bangin' — Jesus already paid the price for the greatest sin you can ever imagine.

Regardless of what you are going through or where you sit today, you are still made righteous through the faithfulness of God. And if you will hold onto your identity, God will treat you as He has identified you. And He will create in you a clean heart and renew a right spirit within you (Read Psalm 51:10).

Grace Walk Prayer
Lord, I am overwhelmed with gratitude that You have called me righteous. I accept who You say I am, and I reject who the enemies of my life say I am. I thank You Lord for these twenty-one days. It is my prayer to You, that You will continue speaking to me and when I forget who You say I am, that You remind me. In Jesus' name, I pray. Amen.

Grace Walk Thoughts

If I can believe that I am righteous, what would that do for how I see myself?

LET US PRAY

*P*raise God! We have spent the last three weeks together and we are hopeful that you are growing with us in our knowledge and belief that God absolutely loves and adores you. Your future in Christ is so bright we need shades (LOL). Seriously, there is such joy in being God's child and we hope that has come through in every single devotion we have shared.

Please join us in a prayer.

Dear Lord, because nothing in You is by chance or coincidence, we know there is a reason why this book reached my hands. I thank You that Your love for me will see me through every moment of my life. I thank You that I am able to face every challenge that comes my way, armed with Your armor, my Helper, and my guardian angels. I thank You that You ensure that through You, my enemies are defeated. I thank You that daily I am able to hit reset on whatever mistakes I have made, renew my mind, and begin again. I thank You that my words have power and that I choose to use my words to speak a positive life into existence for me. I thank You that You keep watch over my children while I am away. Help my children find their way to the path that You have for them that leads to the good life You want them to live. I thank You that I know I am loved by You. I am forgiven by You. I am an heir with Jesus. My youth is restored. My enemies are defeated. I have peace in the midst of any storm. And that I. Am. Righteous.

In Jesus' majestic, magnificent, all powerful, mighty name, I pray and count the victory as mine. Amen.

Be blessed,
Aaron and Monica

PART IV
YOUR TOOL BAG

You are in a rough place. But we hope by now, you know you are not alone. We have included what we call *Your Tool Bag* to help you in your Grace Walk. We pray these scriptures are a blessing to you as they are a blessing to us. Refer to your "Tools" whenever you need them.

PRAYER OF SALVATION

*I*f you are still resisting giving your life to Christ, then this is the prayer for you. It is simple and it just takes your faith to believe it is real. We encourage you to share this prayer (scripture) with others as you feel led by the Holy Spirit.

Just as Moses lifted up the [bronze] serpent in the desert [on a pole], so must the Son of Man be lifted up [on the cross], so that whoever believes will in Him have eternal life [after physical death and will actually live forever]. For God so [greatly] loved and dearly prized the world, that He [even] gave His [One and] only begotten Son, so that whoever believes and trusts in Him [as Savior] shall not perish but have eternal life. For God did not send the Son into the world to judge and condemn the world [that is, to initiate the final judgment of the world], but that the world might be saved through Him. Whoever believes and has decided to trust in Him [as personal Savior and Lord] is not judged [for this one, there is no judgment, no rejection, no condemnation]; but the one who does not believe [and has decided to reject Him as personal Savior and Lord] is judged already [that one has been convicted and sentenced], because he has not believed and trusted in the Name of the [One and]

*only begotten Son of God [the One who is truly unique, the only One of
His kind, the One who alone can save him].*
John 3:14-18 (AMP)

LEARN TO EMBRACE YOUR QUIET TIME

*E*ver spend time by yourself and the silence is louder than being in the middle of a concert? All of us have been there, but it is in those quiet moments that we are able to hear God best.

Learning how to embrace your alone time with our Lord is invaluable. It is during these times that you will begin (or continue) building your relationship with God and the Holy Spirit. Allow your mouth to pour out what your heart is feeling. Why? Because He's listening. He hears you. He will begin to show you how to rid your soul of your deepest hurts and pains.

Believe it or not, there is a blessing in this time that few others will experience. You are purging your mind of distractions so you can focus on God.

Come and listen, all who honor God, and I will tell you what He has done for me. I cried to Him for help; I praised Him with songs. If I had ignored my sins, the Lord would not have listened to me. But God has indeed heard me; He has listened to my prayer. I praise God, because He did not reject my prayer or keep back His constant love from me.
Psalm 66:16-20 (GNT)

WORDS OF PROTECTION

*T*hroughout the Bible, there are promises of God's protection. The deeper you go into God's Word, the more you will find yourself gravitating to certain scriptures. When it comes to protection, our "go to" promise is Psalm 91.

He who dwells in the shelter of the Most High will remain secure and
rest in the shadow of the Almighty [whose power no enemy can
withstand]. I will say of the LORD, "He is my refuge and my fortress,
My God, in whom I trust [with great confidence, and on whom I rely]!"
For He will save you from the trap of the fowler, And from the deadly
pestilence. He will cover you and completely protect you with His
pinions, And under His wings you will find refuge; His faithfulness is a
shield and a wall. You will not be afraid of the terror of night, Nor of
the arrow that flies by day, Nor of the pestilence that stalks in darkness,
Nor of the destruction (sudden death) that lays waste at noon. A
thousand may fall at your side And ten thousand at your right hand,
But danger will not come near you. You will only [be a spectator as you]
look on with your eyes And witness the [divine] repayment of the wicked
[as you watch safely from the shelter of the Most High]. Because you
have made the LORD, [who is] my refuge, Even the Most High, your

dwelling place, No evil will befall you, Nor will any plague come near your tent. For He will command His angels in regard to you, To protect and defend and guard you in all your ways [of obedience and service]. They will lift you up in their hands, So that you do not [even] strike your foot against a stone. You will tread upon the lion and cobra; The young lion and the serpent you will trample underfoot. Because he set his love on Me, therefore I will save him; I will set him [securely] on high, because he knows My name [he confidently trusts and relies on Me, knowing I will never abandon him, no, never]. He will call upon Me, and I will answer him; I will be with him in trouble; I will rescue him and honor him. With a long life I will satisfy him And I will let him see My salvation.
Psalms 91:1-16 (AMP)

Lord, we come to You as Your children, thanking You for bringing us safely through another day. Thank You for loving and protecting us even though we've done nothing to deserve it. Please continue to bless us and keep us protected. In Jesus' name, we pray. Amen.

YOUR ANGELS

*W*e wrote about angels in week one. Here are a few scriptures to study that tell you how angels are here to protect you.

For He shall give His angels charge over you, To keep you in all your ways. In their hands they shall bear you up, Lest you dash your foot against a stone.
Psalms 91:11-12 (NKJV)

When he had come near the den, he called out to Daniel with a troubled voice. The king said to Daniel, "O Daniel, servant of the living God, has your God, whom you constantly serve, been able to rescue you from the lions?" Then Daniel spoke to the king, "O king, live forever! My God has sent His angel and has shut the mouths of the lions so that they have not hurt me, because I was found innocent before Him; and also before you, O king, I have committed no crime." Then the king was greatly pleased and ordered that Daniel be taken out of the den. So Daniel was taken out of the den, and no injury whatever was found on him, because he believed in and relied on and trusted in his God.
Daniel 6:20-23 (AMP)

Behold, I am going to send an Angel before you to keep and guard you on the way and to bring you to the place I have prepared.

When My Angel goes before you and brings you to [the land of] the Amorite, the Hittite, the Perizzite, the Canaanite, the Hivite, and the Jebusite, I will reject them and completely destroy them.
Exodus 23:20, 23 (AMP)

The angel of the LORD encamps around those who fear Him [with awe-inspired reverence and worship Him with obedience], And He rescues [each of] them.
Psalm 34:7 (AMP)

PSALM 23

*W*e encourage you to meditate on Psalm 23 anytime you are feeling weary.

> *The Lord is my shepherd;*
> *I have everything I need.*
> *He lets me rest in fields of green grass*
> *and leads me to quiet pools of fresh water.*
> *He gives me new strength.*
> *He guides me in the right paths,*
> *as He has promised.*
> *Even if I go through the deepest darkness,*
> *I will not be afraid, Lord,*
> *for you are with me.*
> *Your shepherd's rod and staff protect me.*
> *You prepare a banquet for me,*
> *where all my enemies can see me;*
> *You welcome me as an honored guest*
> *and fill my cup to the brim.*

I know that your goodness and love will be with me all my life;
and your house will be my home as long as I live.
Psalms 23:1-6 (GNT)

GREAT BIBLICAL FIGURES WHO DID AWFUL THINGS

*D*id you know that there were some amazing Biblical people who did some awful things, and yet, God still loved them and favored them?

King David - What commandment didn't he break? In 1 and 2 Samuel, we learn that he committed murder, adultery, and stole another man's wife. And yet, God used David to lead His people during a difficult time.

The Apostle Paul - Before he was Paul, he was Saul, and his job was to terrorize and kill Christians. God used Paul to write more than half of the New Testament.

Moses - Killed an Egyptian who was beating a Hebrew slave, then buried him in the sand. God used Moses to lead two million Israelites out of Egypt.

Tamar - Dressed as a prostitute and coerced her father-in-law into having sex with her. She bore twins and one of them was in the lineage of King David, which makes him part of the direct lineage of Jesus Christ.

Did God want them to sin? Of course not. Are we showing you this, so you take comfort in your sin? Nope. We want you to know that there is nothing that you have ever done or could do that would make God love you less. He wants you to live a holy life, and He will still love you when you make mistakes.

THE WHOLE ARMOR OF GOD

*E*very day put on the armor that God gives you and you will be able to defeat every evil thing that comes against you!

Put on all the armor that God gives you, so that you will be able to stand up against the devil's evil tricks.
For we are not fighting against human beings but against the wicked spiritual forces in the heavenly world, the rulers, authorities, and cosmic powers of this dark age.
So put on God's armor now! Then when the evil day comes, you will be able to resist the enemy's attacks; and after fighting to the end, you will still hold your ground.
So stand ready, with truth as a belt tight around your waist, with righteousness as your breastplate,
and as your shoes the readiness to announce the Good News of peace.
At all times carry faith as a shield; for with it you will be able to put out all the burning arrows shot by the Evil One.
And accept salvation as a helmet, and the word of God as the sword which the Spirit gives you.

Do all this in prayer, asking for God's help. Pray on every occasion, as the Spirit leads. For this reason keep alert and never give up; pray always for all God's people.
Ephesians 6:11-18 (GNT)

MUST HAVES FOR YOUR PLAYLIST

$\mathcal{E}$ver listen to music that evokes a response in you? Listen to gangsta rap and feel invincible? Listen to country and wanna have a beer on the back porch with your girl? Throw on some 80s hip hop and get your workout on? There is something about music that touches our soul in both positive and negative ways.

I (Monica) remember years ago leaving a basketball game and listening to something hardcore while my friend and I were in the traffic jam trying to exit the parking lot. Someone walking bumped my car and I went hood on them. It's like it came out of nowhere. My friend looked at me and immediately turned the music to smooth jazz. LOL

Here are some of our favorites that will encourage you and hopefully put a smile on your face and in your heart.

- Love Theory - *Kirk Franklin*
- Your Love - *William Murphy*
- Good Good Father - *Chris Tomlin*
- Break Every Chain - *Jesus Culture*
- Haven't Seen It Yet - *Danny Gokey*

- Nobody Like You Lord - *Maranda Curtis*
- Spirit of the Living God - *Vertical Worship*
- Your Spirit - *Tasha Cobbs ft Kierra Sheard*
- I'm Getting Ready - *Tasha Cobbs ft Nicki Minaj*
- You Know My Name - *Tasha Cobbs ft Jimi Cravity*

ABOUT THE AUTHORS

Aaron and Monica are a brother and sister team who are blessed to be part of a strong, supportive, loving Christian family. Together, they have decided to take the phrase "when life gives you lemons, make lemonade" to another level. They are using the Word of God to spread the message of God's grace to all who need it!

facebook.com/authormonicalynnefoster
twitter.com/authormlfoster
instagram.com/authormonicalynnefoster